WELCOME TO COLORING: SUPPLIES

You can use any medium to color the designs in this book—markers, colored pencils, pens, gel pens, etc. It's all about what YOU love to use! Have fun experimenting with different mediums and brands. My favorite coloring supplies are colored pencils, pencil sharpeners, and erasers.

Colored pencils. I like to use pencils with both hard and soft leads. Pencils with soft leads are great for filling in large areas and blending. Pencils with hard leads achieve crisp, clean lines, making them excellent for detail work and filling in small spaces. Over the years, I have collected a variety of colored pencil brands. I encourage you to experiment with different brands until you find one (or more!) that you really love to work with. I keep my pencils separated into color groups. This allows me to quickly see the range of light and dark shades I have for each color.

Pencil sharpeners. Because I love working with colored pencils, I need a great pencil sharpener. Just like with my pencils, I use more than one type of pencil sharpener depending on the type of point I want to have. I use different points on my pencils depending on the effect I'm trying to create. If you are just starting out, find a sharpener that will give your pencil a strong, sharp point. If you discover you love working with colored pencils as much as I do, you might want to experiment with a few different sharpeners to create different points. Remember that pencils with softer leads are more difficult to sharpen to a fine point than their hard lead counterparts, so be patient!

Erasers. These are helpful for correcting mistakes and smudges or for adding highlights by lifting off some of the color. I like to use a pencil-style eraser that works like a mechanical pencil, allowing me to "click" out more of the eraser as I need it. For big spaces, I use a more traditional block eraser.

CREATIVE PROCESS: HOW MY ART BECOMES A COLORING PAGE

My creative process can start with anything from a phrase or a word to a feeling or an image! I focus on that inspiration and use it to develop a rough sketch. The sketch allows me to decide how I want to put the word or image and the rest of the artwork together.

Sometimes, a sketch inspires me to create another piece of art, like a mixed-media painting! If you are inspired by one of these coloring pages, don't be afraid to take it out of the book! Frame your art, decoupage it onto a canvas or wood surface, or use it for another craft project.

If I'm planning to turn the design into a coloring page, I redraw it in ink and add patterning. I designed fabric for years, which has given me lots of patterns to use in my coloring designs!

Once I am happy with the ink design and patterning, I import it to my computer as a digital image. Through the magic of my computer and design software, I'm able to turn the design into chalkboard art by adding a black chalkboard background and changing some of the black lines to white.

Once I've finalized the design on the computer, the real fun begins... I get to start coloring! For "Dream Big!", I knew I wanted a limited color palette using mostly cool colors and only a few warm colors to add some pop. When I'm finished coloring, I get to share my design with you!

Every design starts out as a rough pencil sketch that can be inspired by almost anything!

Sometimes a design needs to come off the page and transform into something else, like this mixed-media painting. If inspiration grabs you, follow it!

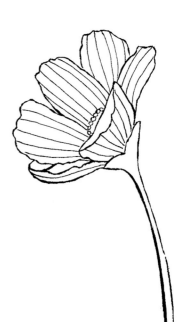

To turn a sketch into a coloring page, I redraw it in ink and add patterning. I take lots of inspiration from my years as a fabric designer.

When the design is ready, it's imported to the computer and turned into chalkboard art through the addition of a chalky black background.

I love when I get to color my finished design.

And I love sharing the finished product with you!

HERE ARE SOME
MORE EXAMPLES OF ART
(CHALKBOARD AND MORE!)
THAT I HAVE CREATED!

He Is
Risen

Christ the
Lord
is risen
today
Alleluia
Alleluia

SING
YOUR
SONG

HAPPY
EASTER

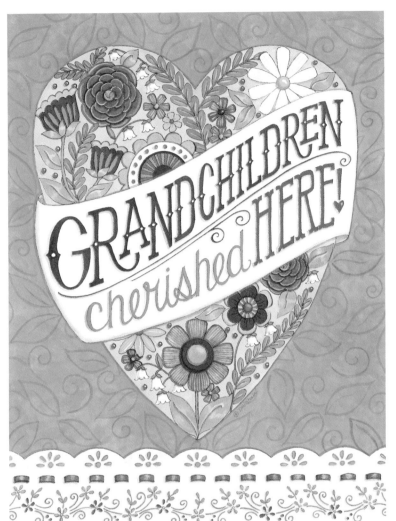

COLOR THEORY

Picking the colors you want to use for a design can be intimidating, but it doesn't have to be! Some basic understanding of color theory will go a long way toward making you feel more comfortable about choosing colors. Ultimately, though, it's good to remember that there is no right way or wrong way to color a design in this book, so don't be afraid to dive in!

It all starts with the primary colors red, yellow, and blue. These three colors can be mixed to create a whole rainbow, but they cannot be created by mixing other colors—this is why they are "primary." If you mix two primary colors, you will get the secondary colors orange (red + yellow), green (yellow + blue), and purple (blue + red). Mixing a primary color and a secondary color will result in a tertiary color. These include yellow-orange, yellow-green, blue-green, blue-purple, red-purple, and red-orange. Any primary, secondary, or tertiary color can be darkened or

lightened by the addition of white or black. The result is a tint or shade of the original color. For example, pink is a tint of red created by adding white, and burgundy is a shade of red created by adding black.

Take a look at the color wheel. It is your most helpful tool when it comes to understanding how colors relate to one another. Think of the color wheel as having two sides. On one side are the warm colors yellow, orange, and red. On the other side are the cool colors green, blue, and purple. Warm colors are bold and evoke excitement. They will pop out of your design, especially when paired with cool colors. Cool colors are calm and evoke relaxation and peacefulness. They will recede in a design. Warm colors will always pair well with one another, and cool colors will always pair well with one another.

Another handy color relationship you should be aware of is analogous colors. Analogous colors are next to

one another on the color wheel. One reason warm colors and cool colors go well together is because they are analogous, but you don't have to limit yourself to warm and cool colors only. A mix of warm and cool analogous colors will make a great color scheme. For example, blue and green (both cool) pair well with yellow (warm).

One final color relationship for your arsenal is complementary colors. Complementary colors are directly opposite one another on the color wheel. If you look at the color wheel, you'll see that all complementary pairings contain a warm and a cool color. For example, orange (warm) and blue (cool). As their name suggests, complementary colors "complement" one another. They also stand out against one another more than they do against any other color. You can use this relationship to create some real impact!

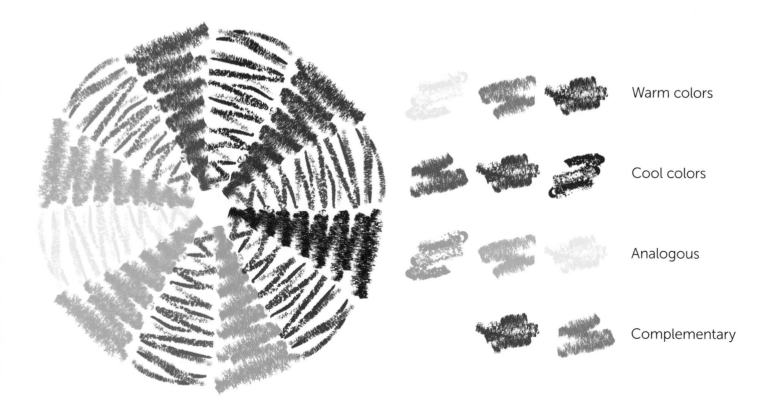

Warm colors

Cool colors

Analogous

Complementary

TIPS AND TRICKS FOR CHALKBOARD ART

The black chalkboard background used for these pieces adds another element to consider when coloring. Here are some tips and tricks that you might find helpful.

Use strong colors. This doesn't necessarily mean that you need to use bright colors, just ones with strong saturation (that don't look washed out). You may have to apply two or three layers of a color to create a rich, strong appearance. You'll want your colors to have this intensity so they stand out against the black chalkboard background, making the colored area the focal point rather than the chalkboard.

Plan ahead. Think about the colors you'd like to use before you start coloring. You might want to use colors from one color family, like cool colors or warm colors. Areas colored with cool colors tend to recede. To make areas pop or stand out, accent them with a color from another color family. For example, warm colors will stand out against cool colors. Using colors primarily from one color group with only accents from another group will give your finished piece a cohesive appearance. If you want a fun, vibrant look—go crazy! Use colors from a variety of color families.

Leave some lines. You can also use the black lines that are already part of the design to add to your patterns and create definition. Leaving some black showing within colored areas helps tie in or balance the black background.

Black and white are colors, too! Because you are working on a black background, white will stand out against it the most. If you want a certain area to stand out, or if you are worried about a particularly fine detail getting lost, then leave it white. For example, as you can see, I left some of the areas on the butterflies' wings white.

COLOR INSPIRATION

One of my favorite things about creating a new piece of art is coloring it and sharing it with you. The following pages are filled with colored samples from this book to get you thinking and imagining about all of the things you can do with the designs. As you look at them, take mental note of the color schemes you enjoy. I hope these pieces inspire you before you sit down to color your own beautiful art in your unique style!

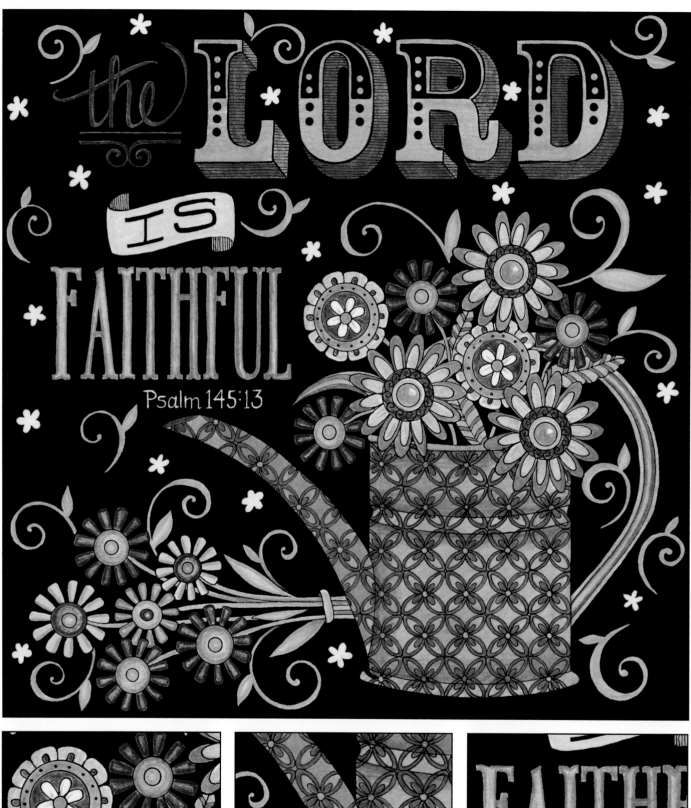

the LORD IS FAITHFUL

Psalm 145:13

FAITHF

Psalm 14

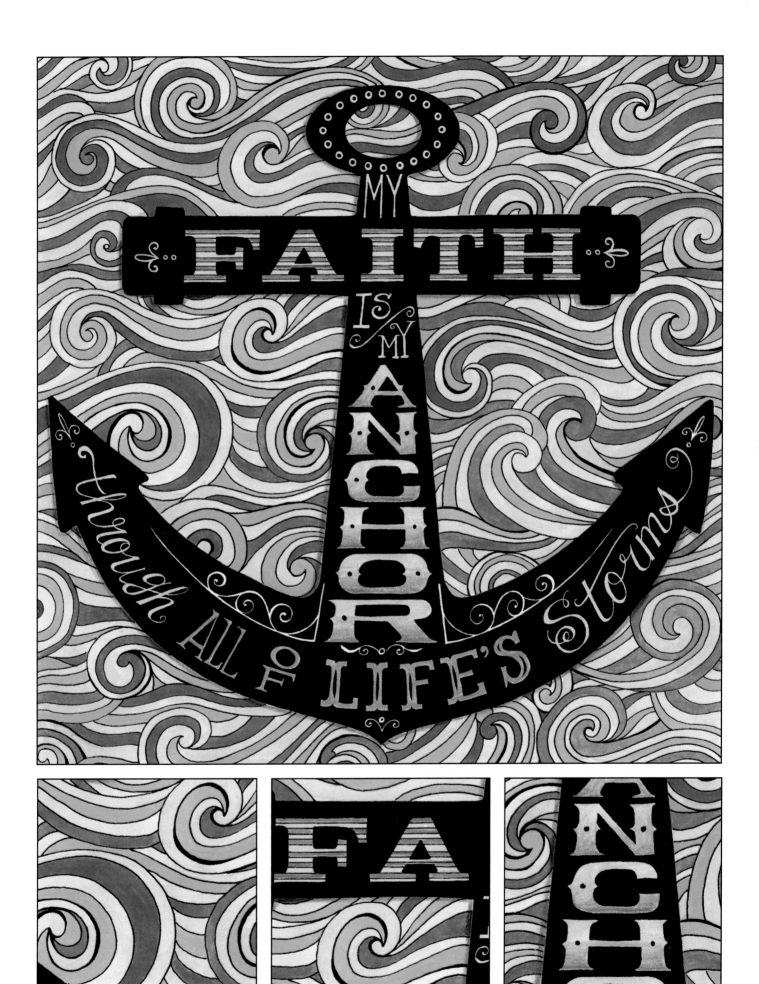

BE JOYFUL Always

1 Thessalonians 5:16

To be grateful is to recognize
the love of God in everything
He has given us—and
He has given us everything.

—Thomas Merton

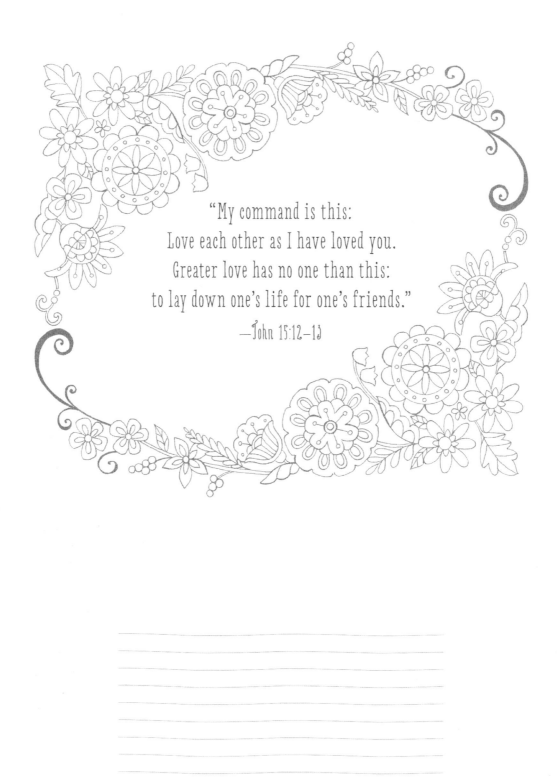

"My command is this:
Love each other as I have loved you.
Greater love has no one than this:
to lay down one's life for one's friends."

—John 15:12–13

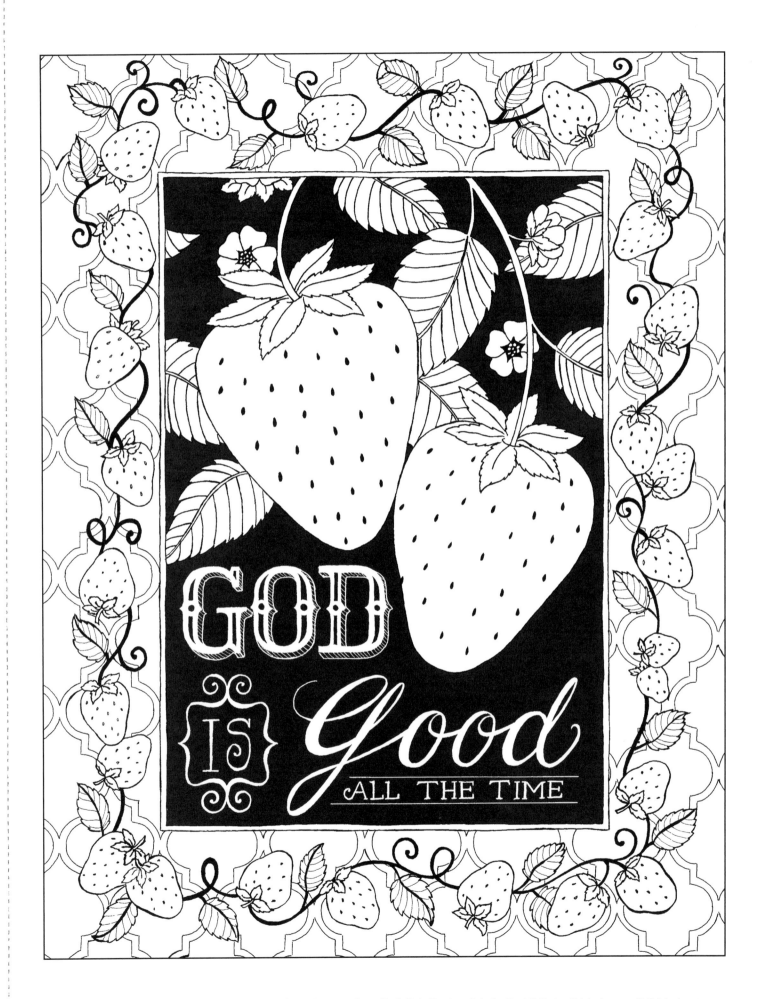

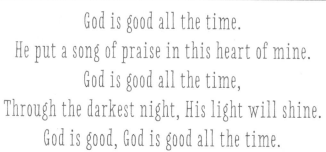

God is good all the time.
He put a song of praise in this heart of mine.
God is good all the time,
Through the darkest night, His light will shine.
God is good, God is good all the time.

—Don Moen

God Is Good

In daily life we must see that it is not happiness that
makes us grateful, but gratefulness that makes us happy.

—David Steindl-Rast

Give Thanks

LIFE IS *Fragile* HANDLE WITH PRAYER

Devote yourselves to prayer,
being watchful and thankful.

—Colossians 4:2

Fear can keep us up all night long,
but faith makes one fine pillow.

—*Philip Gulley*

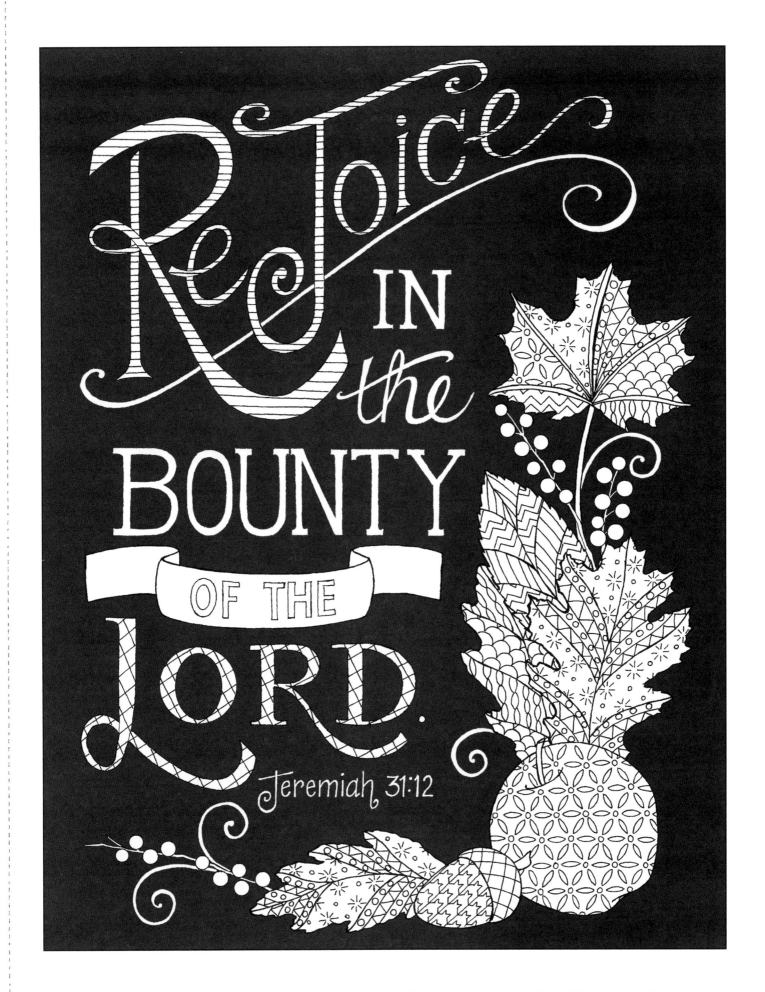

All things bright and beautiful,
All creatures great and small,
All things wise and wonderful:
The Lord God made them all.

—Cecil Frances Alexander

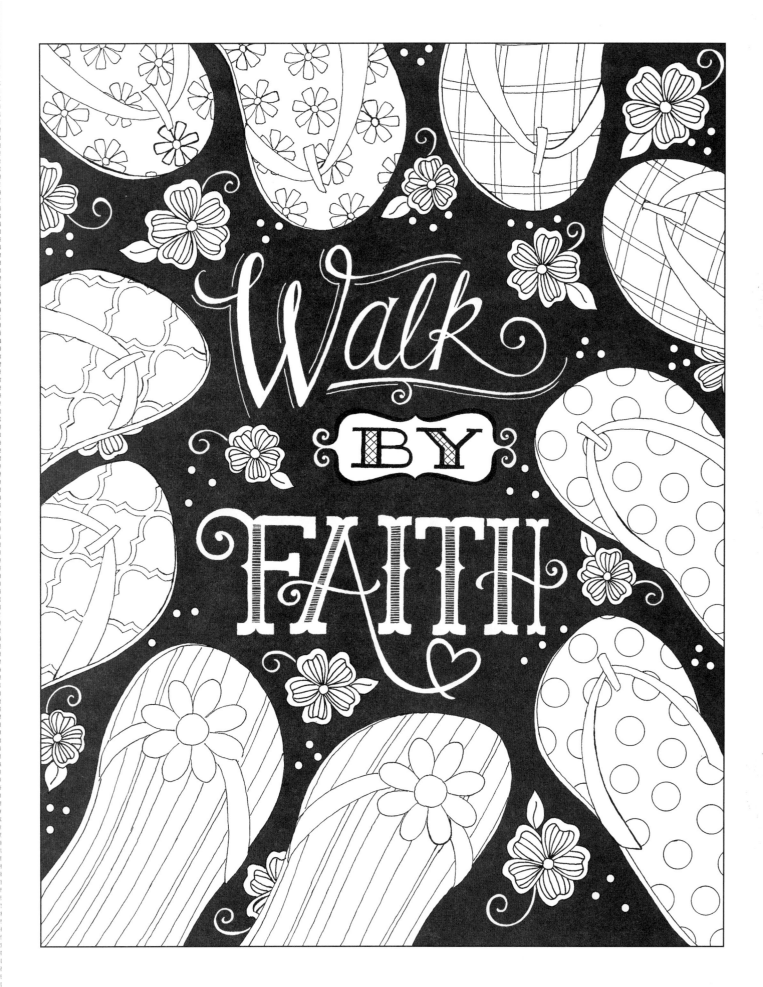

Walk BY FAITH

Faith is about doing. You are how you act,
not just how you believe.

—Mitch Albom

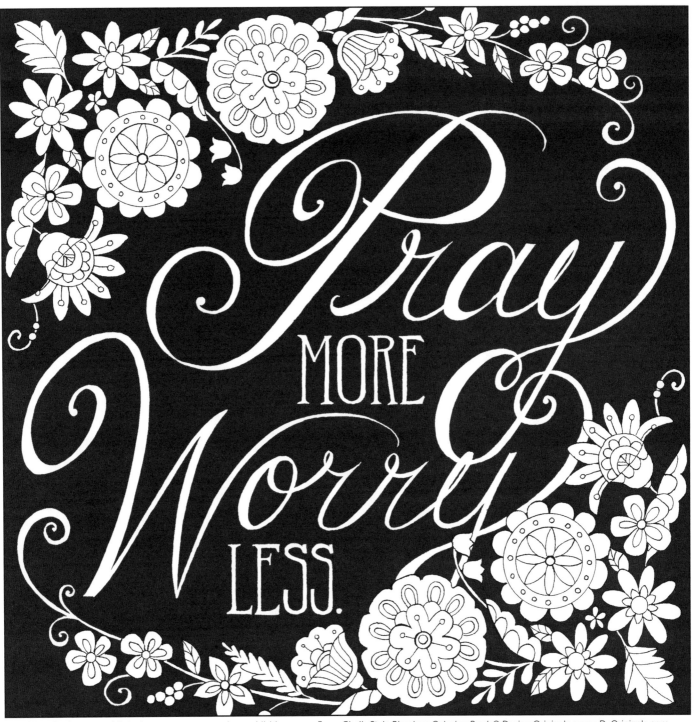

Try an analogous color scheme of pinks, oranges, and reds for a warm, cohesive feel.

No one can pray and worry at the same time.

—Max Lucado

Worry Not

Cool blues stand out when framed by warm pink words.

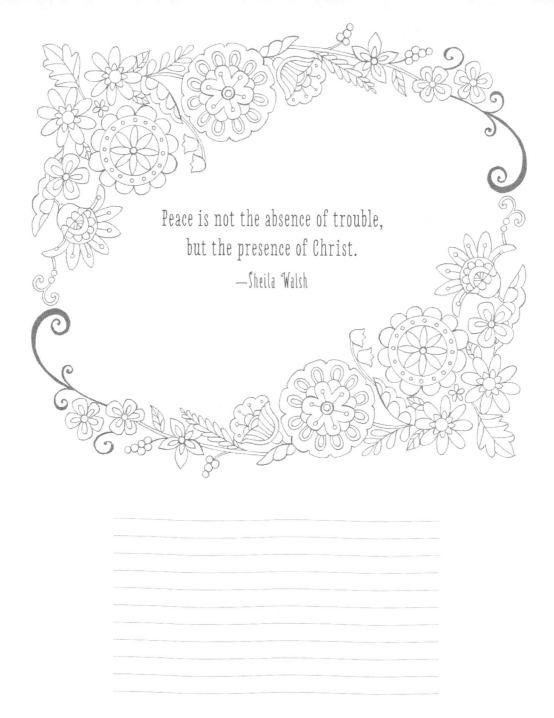

Peace is not the absence of trouble,
but the presence of Christ.

—Sheila Walsh

Stress Free

You don't need to color every part of the art! Leave some words and some parts of the pattern blank.

See what great love the Father has lavished on us,
that we should be called children of God!

—1 John 3:1

Tree of Values

the LORD IS FAITHFUL

Psalm 145:13

Press harder with your colored pencils to create instant shading, as seen on this watering can.

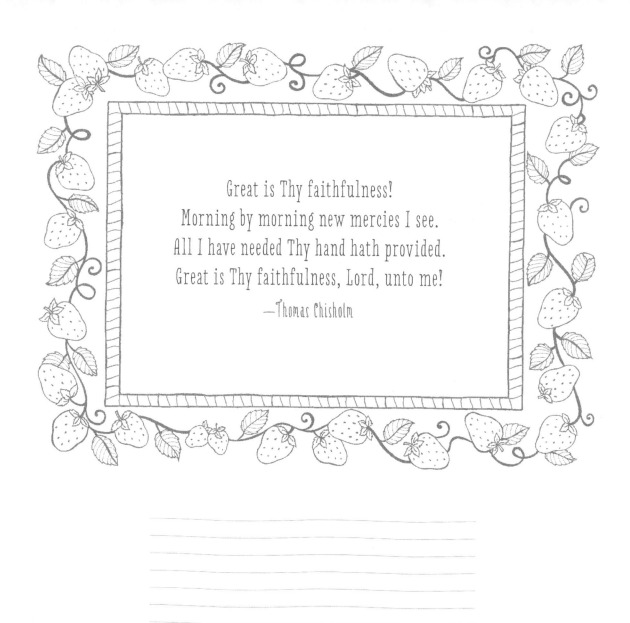

Great is Thy faithfulness!
Morning by morning new mercies I see.
All I have needed Thy hand hath provided.
Great is Thy faithfulness, Lord, unto me!

—Thomas Chisholm

Faithful Flowers

Bright oranges will pop against a literal sea of blues.

Now faith is the assurance of things hoped for, the conviction of things not seen.

—Hebrews 11:1

Anchored

Complementary yellow and purple create a festive mood that perfectly fits the sentiment expressed in this art.

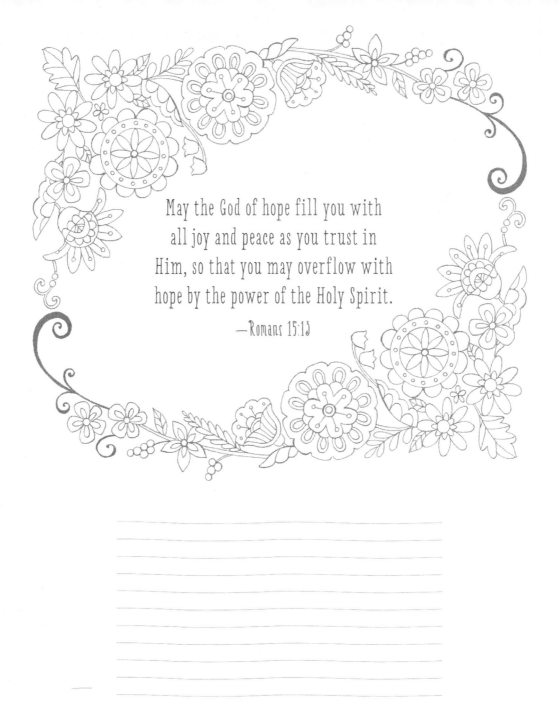

May the God of hope fill you with
all joy and peace as you trust in
Him, so that you may overflow with
hope by the power of the Holy Spirit.

—Romans 15:13

_____
_____
_____
_____
_____
_____
_____
_____
_____
_____

Always Joyful

Try coloring a piece of art with realistic colors—like the yellow daisy, red ladybugs, and green leaves here—to take advantage of natural beauty.

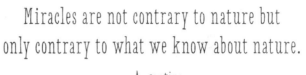

Miracles are not contrary to nature but
only contrary to what we know about nature.

—Augustine

_____
_____
_____
_____
_____
_____
_____
_____
_____
_____

Miracles

Use every shade of blue in your collection, and add some splashes of green to keep it interesting.

Do not be anxious about anything,
but in every situation,
by prayer and petition,
with thanksgiving,
present your requests to God.

—Philippians 4:6

Prayer Advice

These three remain: faith, hope, and love.
But the greatest of these is love.

—1 Corinthians 13:13

EVERY GOOD AND PERFECT *Gift* IS FROM ABOVE

James 1:17

God cannot give us a happiness
and peace apart from Himself,
because it is not there.
There is no such thing.

—C. S. Lewis

Praise God from whom all blessings flow;
Praise Him, all creatures here below;
Praise Him above, ye heavenly host;
Praise Father, Son, and Holy Ghost. Amen.

—Thomas Ken

Rejoice

AND BE GLAD! Matt. 5:12

This is the day that the LORD has made;
let us rejoice and be glad in it.

—Psalm 118:24

_____

_____

_____

_____

_____

_____

_____

_____

There is a TIME FOR EVERYTHING

and a season for every activity under heaven:

ECCLESIASTES 3:1

God does not give us everything we want,
but He does fulfill His promises, leading us
along the best and straightest paths to Himself.

—Dietrich Bonhoeffer

God loves each of us as if
there were only one of us.

—Augustine

Put your trust in God and just calmly go your way.

—Norman Vincent Peale

_____

_____

_____

_____

_____

_____

_____

_____

WHEN *Life* is TOUGH, PRAY
WHEN *Life* is GREAT, PRAY

To pray is to listen also, to move through my own chattering to God, to that place where I can be silent and listen to what God may have to say.

—Madeleine L'Engle

Amazing grace! How sweet the sound
That saved a wretch like me!
I once was lost, but now am found;
Was blind, but now I see.

—John Newton

Create IN ME A PURE heart

Of all earthly music, that which
reaches farthest into heaven is the
beating of a truly loving heart.

—Henry Ward Beecher

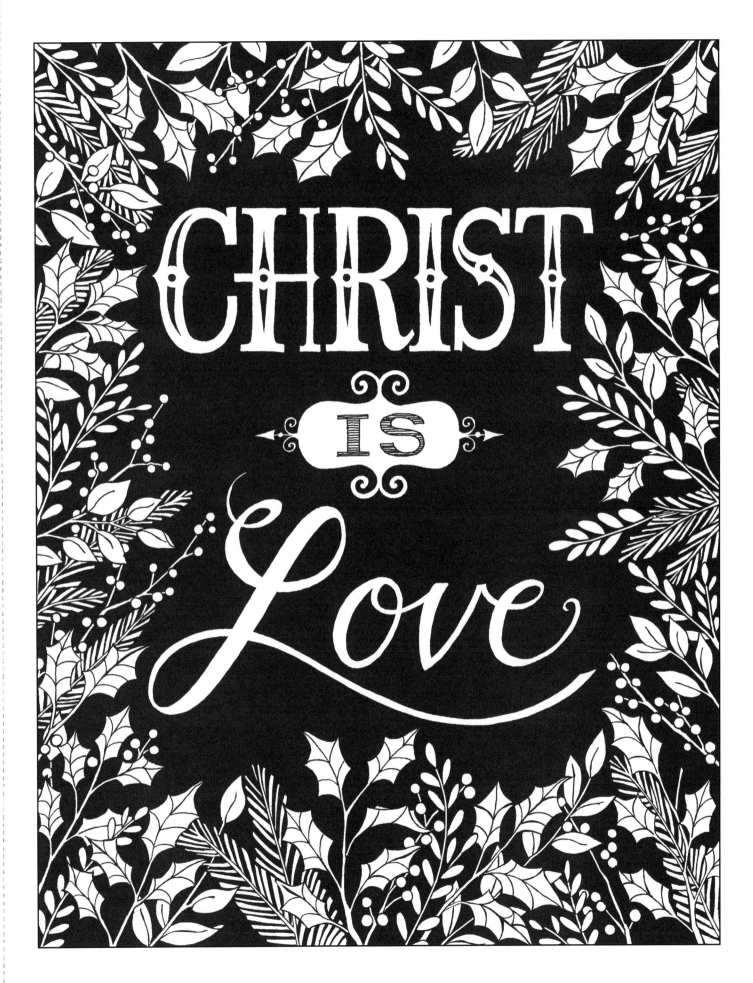

God is love. He didn't need us.
But He wanted us. And that is the most amazing thing.

—Rick Warren

Love

Be sure that you never try to work God into your schedule, but always work your schedule around Him.

—Joyce Meyer

_____
_____
_____
_____
_____
_____
_____
_____
_____
_____

HEM

YOUR BLESSINGS WITH *Thankfulness*

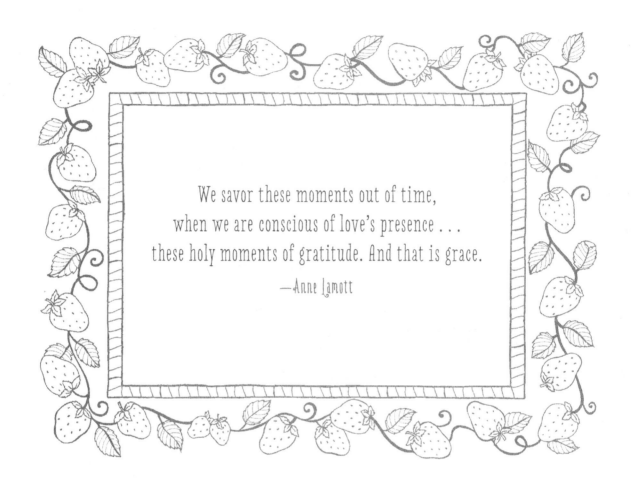

We savor these moments out of time,
when we are conscious of love's presence . . .
these holy moments of gratitude. And that is grace.

—Anne Lamott

God is love. Therefore love.
Without distinction, without calculation,
without procrastination, love.

—Henry Drummond

Love All

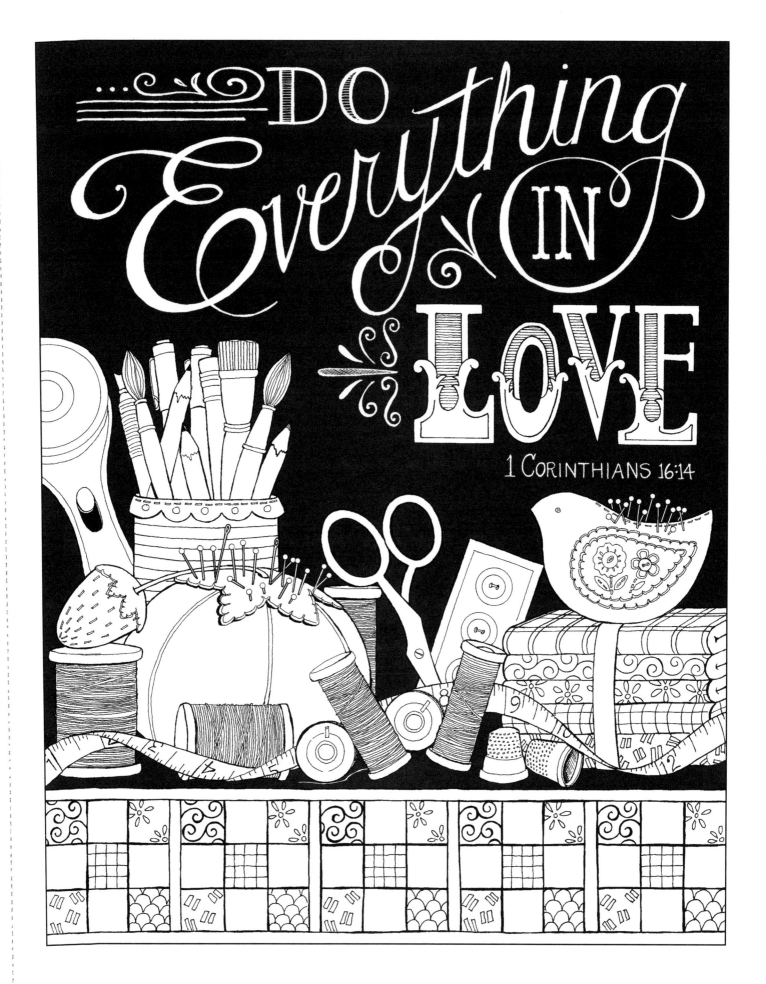

Do Everything IN LOVE

1 Corinthians 16:14

Go out on a limb when you pray for others.
Take a risk. Be outrageous. Be passionate.
Take a leap. Love a lot, not just a little.

—Rick Hamlin

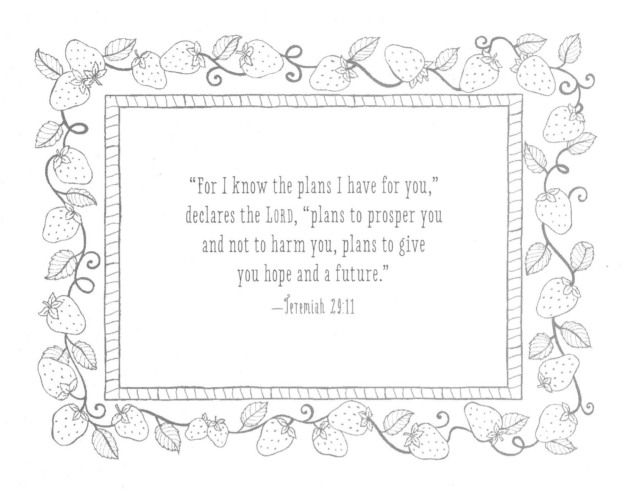

"For I know the plans I have for you,"
declares the LORD, "plans to prosper you
and not to harm you, plans to give
you hope and a future."

—Jeremiah 29:11